AUSTRALIA

Julie Murray

Big Buddy BOOKS
Explore the Countries

VISIT US AT
www.abdopublishing.com

Published by ABDO Publishing Company, PO Box 398166, Minneapolis, MN 55439.

Copyright © 2014 by Abdo Consulting Group, Inc. International copyrights reserved in all countries. No part of this book may be reproduced in any form without written permission from the publisher. Big Buddy Books™ is a trademark and logo of ABDO Publishing Company.

Printed in the United States of America, North Mankato, Minnesota.
042013
092013

 PRINTED ON RECYCLED PAPER

Coordinating Series Editor: Rochelle Baltzer
Contributing Editors: Megan M. Gunderson, Marcia Zappa
Graphic Design: Adam Craven
Cover Photograph: *Shutterstock*: Debra James.
Interior Photographs/Illustrations: *AP Photo*: Bryce Barker (p. 13), North Wind Picture Archives via AP Images (p. 15), Press Association via AP Images (p. 17); *Getty Images*: Auscape/UIG (p. 35), Vince Caligiuri (p. 29), Hulton Archive (p. 31), Jon Kopaloff/FilmMagic (p. 33), Mark Metcalfe (p. 33), Quinn Rooney (p. 29), Rick Rycroft-Pool (p. 19), Pawel Toczynski (p. 21); *Glow Images*: Karl Johaentges/LOOK-foto (p. 35), The Print Collector (p. 13); *iStockphoto*: ©iStockphoto.com/miralex (p. 37); *Shutterstock*: Steven Bostock (p. 34), Robyn Butler (p. 23), edella (p. 5), Martin Froyda (p. 16), Globe Turner (pp. 19, 38), Damian Herde (p. 34), Chris Howey (p. 9), jabiru (pp. 11, 27), Phillip Minnis (p. 38), Pete Niesen (p. 35), Perig (p. 11), ruchos (p. 25), SF photo (p. 9), solarseven (p. 23), worldswildlifewonders (p. 23).

Country population and area figures taken from the CIA World Factbook.

Library of Congress Control Number: 2013932238

Cataloging-in-Publication Data

Tieck, Sarah.
 Australia / Sarah Tieck.
   p. cm. -- (Explore the countries)
 ISBN 978-1-61783-804-0 (lib. bdg.)
 1. Australia--Juvenile literature. I. Title.
 994--dc23
                                                2013932238

AUSTRALIA

Contents

Around the World

Our world has many countries. Each country has beautiful land. It has its own rich history. And, the people have their own languages and ways of life.

Australia is the only country that is also a **continent**. What do you know about Australia? Let's learn more about this place and its story!

Did You Know?

English is the official language of Australia.

Australia is the only country that is also a **continent**.

<u>Bold</u> word: continent.
<u>Find definition in:</u>
~~Glossary~~/index

Australia is known for the outback. This land includes many deserts. It covers about 75 to 80 percent of the country.

5

Passport to Australia

Australia is in Earth's southern **hemisphere**. It is an island located between the Indian Ocean and the Pacific Ocean. Australia has six states and two territories.

Australia's total area is 2,988,902 square miles (7,741,220 sq km). More than 22 million people live there.

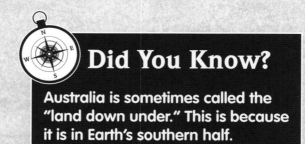

Did You Know?

Australia is sometimes called the "land down under." This is because it is in Earth's southern half.

Australia is in earth's southern **hemisphere.**

<u>Bold word</u>: Hemisphere

<u>Find definition in:</u>

~~Glossary / index.~~

Australia is located beetween the Indian Ocean and the Pacific Ocean.

Australia's Area is 2,988,902 square miles (7,741,220 sq km.)

INDONESIA

PAPUA NEW GUINEA

EAST TIMOR

SOLOMON ISLANDS

INDIAN OCEAN

AUSTRALIA

PACIFIC OCEAN

INDIAN OCEAN

IMPORTANT CITIES

Canberra is Australia's **capital**. More than 323,000 people live there. This city was carefully planned. Building began around 1913. In 1927, the Australian Parliament met there for the first time.

Sydney is Australia's largest city, with more than 4 million people. It is a leader in business. It is on Port Jackson, which is also called Sydney Harbour. Many goods are shipped around the world from this busy port.

Did You Know?

Sydney is Australia's oldest city. It was founded by the British in 1788.

Canberra has hills and grassy land. The Molonglo River flows through the city.

AUSTRALIA

NORTHERN TERRITORY

WESTERN AUSTRALIA

QUEENSLAND

Brisbane

SOUTH AUSTRALIA

NEW SOUTH WALES

Sydney

Canberra

AUSTRALIAN CAPITAL TERRITORY

VICTORIA

Melbourne

TASMANIA

N
W E
S

The Sydney Opera House is famous around the world.

9

Melbourne is Australia's second-largest city. It has about 3.6 million people. This coastal city is on Port Phillip Bay. It is known for its large port and for being a center of business.

Brisbane is Australia's third-largest city, with about 1.8 million people. Many goods are made in and shipped from this city. Visitors spend time on the area's beaches and enjoy the mild weather.

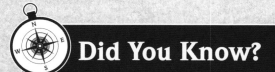

Did You Know?

Brisbane was named for Sir Thomas Brisbane. He was the governor of New South Wales when the area was settled in 1824.

Australia's **Capital** is
 Canberra.

 Bold word: Capital

Canberra was built in 1913.
Sydney is Australia's largest
city. It is on Port Jackson,
which is also called Sydney Harbour.

Melbourne is Australia's second-
largest city.

Melbourne is on the Yarra River. It is known for the arts and for hosting sporting events.

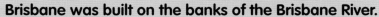

Brisbane was built on the banks of the Brisbane River.

AUSTRALIA IN HISTORY

SAY IT

Aborigines
AB-uh-RIHJ-uh-neez

The first people to live in Australia came from Southeast Asia by boat. They were the ancestors of Australia's native people, the Aborigines.

In the 1600s, the Dutch began exploring what is now Australia. They sailed around western Australia, Tasmania, and New Zealand. In 1770, Captain James Cook arrived. He claimed eastern Australia for Great Britain.

Aboriginal rock art is one of the world's oldest kinds of art. Some dates back about 30,000 years!

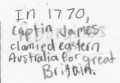

In 1770, captin James clamied eastern Australia for great Britain.

The first people to live in Australia came from Southeast Asia by boat.

Dutch explorer Abel Tasman was the first European to see Tasmania.

Did You Know?

Aborigines created the boomerang as a tool for hunting and war.

In 1788, the British began to settle Australia. They made it into a prison colony. People who had committed crimes were sent there. Other settlers also arrived. By the late 1830s, there were twice as many free settlers as convicts.

In 1851, gold was discovered. As news spread, more people arrived from Great Britain. On January 1, 1901, Australia became a country. Between **World War I** and **World War II**, the people struggled. Later, the government encouraged **immigration**. This helped Australia grow strong.

Did You Know?

Australia's first settlement was at Sydney Cove. It was started on January 26, 1788. That date is now a holiday called Australia Day.

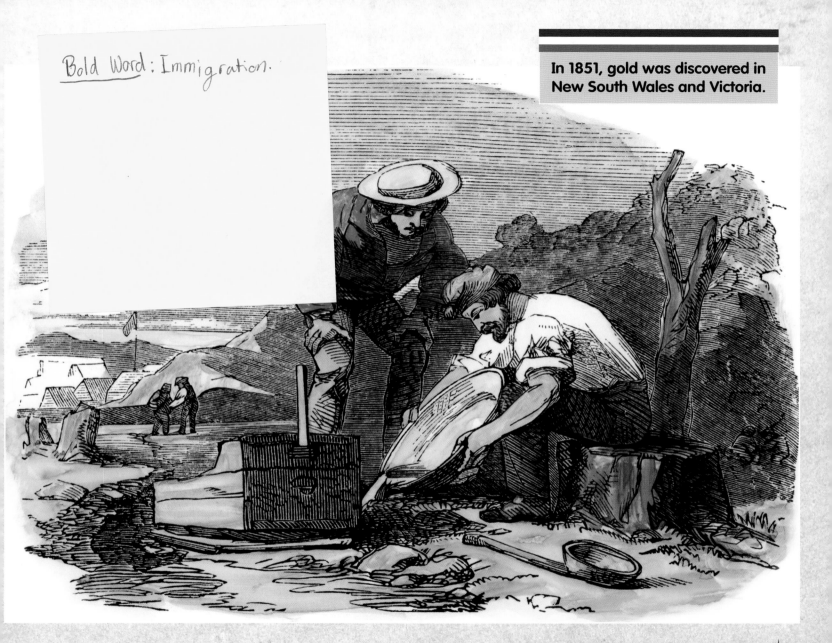

Bold Word: Immigration.

In 1851, gold was discovered in New South Wales and Victoria.

Timeline

1770

Captain James Cook found the Great Barrier **Reef** while exploring Australia. He was the first European to see it. It is so large that it can be seen from outer space!

1895

Poet Banjo Paterson wrote the words to a song called "Waltzing Matilda." It is about a man who travels in the wild carrying his belongings. It is considered Australia's most famous song.

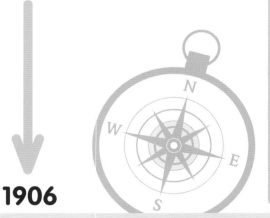

1906

Australia became one of the first countries to make a full-length film. It was called *The Story of the Kelly Gang*.

1956

Melbourne hosted the Summer Olympic Games. This was the first time the Olympics were held in the southern **hemisphere**.

1973

The Sydney Opera House opened. Queen Elizabeth II of the United Kingdom was there for the event.

2010

Julia Gillard became Australia's first female prime minister.

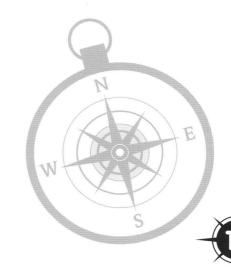

An Important Symbol

Australia's flag was adopted in 1954. A United Kingdom flag is in the upper left corner. The rest is blue with six white stars. The largest star stands for Australia's states and the Northern Territory.

Australia's government is a constitutional monarchy. But, it operates as a **federal parliamentary democracy**. Its parliament has two parts that make laws together. The prime minister is the head of government. The king or queen of the United Kingdom is the head of state.

Queen Elizabeth II (*left*) became Australia's head of state in 1952. A governor-general stands in for the king or queen. Quentin Bryce (*right*) became the governor-general in 2008.

Australia's flag!

On Au
stars s
In Aust
can be

ACROSS THE LAND

Australia is mostly low and flat. Deserts cover about one-third of the land. But, there are also coasts, farmland, forests, and mountains. The Australian Alps are in the southeast. They are home to the country's highest mountains.

Australia is bordered by oceans. The Murray River is one of the longest rivers in the country. Australia also has underground water called artesian water. It is trapped under rock. It gushes out when people drill wells.

Did You Know?

Australia's seasons are opposite of countries in Earth's northern hemisphere. In July, the average temperature in Queensland is 65°F (18°C). In January, it is about 90°F (32°C).

Mount Kosciuszko is Australia's highest peak, at 7,310 feet (2,228 m). It is in the Snowy Mountains, which are part of the Australian Alps.

Many types of animals make their homes in Australia. Thousands of fish and other sea creatures live in the Great Barrier **Reef**. Other Australian animals include emus, wallabies, wombats, kangaroos, koalas, and platypuses.

Australia's land is home to a variety of plants. These include acacias and eucalyptuses. Palm trees, saltbushes, and wildflowers also grow there.

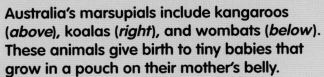

Australia's marsupials include kangaroos (*above*), koalas (*right*), and wombats (*below*). These animals give birth to tiny babies that grow in a pouch on their mother's belly.

Bold word: Reef

Earning a Living

In Australia, most people have service jobs. They work for places such as banks, schools, restaurants, and hotels. Australia's factories process mine and farm products to send around the world.

Australia has many natural **resources**. Mining is an important business there. Coal, copper, opals, and uranium come from Australia. Farmers produce barley, cotton, and grapes. They raise cattle, chicken, hogs, and sheep.

Did You Know?

People around the world use wool from Australia's sheep.

Sheep and cattle graze in Australia's grassy fields.

LIFE IN AUSTRALIA

Most Australians live in modern cities. Others live in the country's **rural** areas, or the "bush." They may work in mines. Or, they may live on farms.

Beef and other meats are popular foods in Australia. Foods from around the world are also eaten there. Tea, coffee, beer, and wine are popular drinks. Australia makes world-famous wines.

Did You Know?

In Australia, children must attend school from ages 6 to 15 or 16.

Bold Word: Rural

Vegemite is an Australian food spread. It has a strong, salty flavor.

Australians enjoy sports. People watch and play cricket. They also enjoy rugby, tennis, and Australian rules football.

Many Australians like to do outdoor activities and water sports. These include boating, diving, swimming, and surfing.

The country is known for its powerful athletes. There are track-and-field stars and top-ranked swimmers. Australia also has strong surfers, golfers, and tennis players.

In Australian rules football, players often tackle the player who has the ball.

The Melbourne Cup is a famous horse race held in November.

FAMOUS FACES

Australia has been home to many famous people. Edward "Ned" Kelly was born around 1855 near Melbourne. He was a famous bushranger, or bandit.

Kelly stole things and killed people during his life. He believed the working people of Australia were treated unfairly. He wrote letters about this. Some people called him a hero. Others considered him a criminal. He died in 1880. People continued to tell his story after his death.

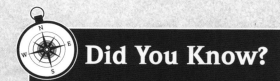

Did You Know?

Ned Kelly's father was from Ireland. He was sent to Australia for committing a crime.

Kelly was part of a group of bandits called the Kelly gang. He was known for wearing a suit of armor made from plow parts.

Steve Irwin was famous for his work with animals. He was born on February 22, 1962, in Essendon, Victoria. He grew up caring for animals at his family's animal park. He later renamed it the Australia Zoo.

In the 1990s, Irwin became the star of *The Crocodile Hunter*. He and his family also ran the Australia Zoo. Sadly, Irwin died in 2006. His wife, Terri, and their children, Bindi and Robert, have continued his work.

Did You Know?

Irwin often said, "Crikey!" This is an Australian expression of surprise.

Irwin was known for his daring with animals. He often got close to animals such as crocodiles and snakes.

Terri, Bindi, and Robert also became television stars.

Tour Book

Have you ever been to Australia? If you visit the country, here are some places to go and things to do!

 See

Spend some time at the Australia Zoo in Beerwah, Queensland. You'll see animals such as koalas and elephants! The zoo is run by the family of Steve Irwin.

 Play

Build a sand castle on one of the warm beaches near Brisbane. Or surf in the ocean! Queensland is known for a line of beaches that make up the Sunshine Coast.

 Explore

Visit the Great Barrier Reef off Australia's northeast coast. People come from around the world to see all its shapes and colors.

Dance

See an Aboriginal dance. Many groups perform traditional music and dances throughout Australia.

Sing

Visit Waltzing Matilda Centre in Winton, Queensland. This museum is about the history of the famous Australian folk song.

A Great Country

The story of Australia is important to our world. The people and places that make up this country offer something special. They help make the world a more beautiful, interesting place.

Ayers Rock, or Uluru, is in the outback in central Australia. It has caves with walls covered in Aboriginal rock carvings and paintings.

Australia Up Close

Official Name: Commonwealth of Australia

Flag:

Population (rank): 22,015,576
(July 2012 est.)
(53rd most-populated country)

Total Area (rank): 2,988,902 square miles
(6th largest country)

Capital: Canberra

Official Language: English

Currency: Australian dollar

Form of Government: Constitutional
monarchy and federal parliamentary
democracy

National Anthem: "Advance Australia Fair"

Important Words

capital a city where government leaders meet.
continent one of Earth's seven main land areas.
federal parliamentary democracy a government in which the power is held by the people, who exercise it by voting. It is run by a cabinet whose members belong to the legislature. The central government and the individual states and territories share power.
hemisphere (HEH-muh-sfihr) one half of the earth.
immigration the act of leaving one's home and settling in a new country.
reef a line of underwater rocks, sand, or coral near the surface of the ocean.
resource a supply of something useful or valued.
rural of or relating to open land away from towns and cities.
World War I a war fought in Europe from 1914 to 1918.
World War II a war fought in Europe, Asia, and Africa from 1939 to 1945.

Web Sites

To learn more about Australia, visit ABDO Publishing Company online. Web sites about Australia are featured on our Book Links page. These links are routinely monitored and updated to provide the most current information available.

www.abdopublishing.com

39

Index